Dedication

This book is dedicated to our 5 children Ryan, Tara, Cory, Jesse and Taylor and their partners and the precious Grands. Your continued presence in our life is a constant source of joy and the Grands inspire me to better see the world through their eyes.
Love Mama Dukes/Your Wicked Stepmother/Nana.

© 2024 Brenda Louise Pritchard born in 1958.
All rights reserved.

I would like to thank all of the amazing reference photographers and a professional tour guide who shared their images and stories with me including Jane Pritchard, Ken McKeen, Craig Cameron, Diane Cameron, Victoria Foley, Jenni Evans, Heather Harris and Joan Taylor.

Creative Direction:
Linda Glendenning, LINLEE
Instagram: @linleesocialmedia

introduction

My name is Whisky the Portuguese Water Dog and this summer
I am turning five years old. My Mom and I love telling stories of the
wonderful animals we have seen and Mom has painted.

This time we decided to go to the special group of islands called Galapagos.
In Spanish Galapagos means "saddle" and the islands were named for the giant
tortoises whose hard shell looks like a riding saddle. These islands are made
up of volcanic lava rock formed by volcanic eruptions off the coast
of Ecuador in South America.

This area became famous after a young explorer named Charles Darwin
travelled there by ship in 1835 and studied the unique animals and birds that
seem to have adapted over time depending on the harsh climatic conditions.
Mr. Darwin published the book "On the Origin of Species" that became
very important in the scientific world.

TOMAS THE TORTOISE

Land of the Giant Tortoises

The Galapagos Giant Tortoises are among the largest in the world weighing up to 900 pounds and also the longest living, with some living 175 years. You can see me beside Tomas the Tortoise on the cover of this book. What is important to the origin of species is that from island to island only about 40 miles apart, over time they adapted to the specific conditions so that the tortoises from one island could be very different from another. On islands with dry lowlands, the tortoises are smaller with "saddleback" shells and long necks. On other islands with more humid conditions, the tortoises are much larger with domed shells and short necks and live in larger groups.

The idea is that over time the tortoises that were most successful in staying alive would be most likely to breed successfully and have more babies. Over time they started to look quite different. I like to think that as a Portuguese Water Dog whose ancestors helped the fishermen fill their nets with fish, our breed develop webbed feet and very strong paws and jaws that helped us become great fishermen.

You Scratch My Back I'll Scratch Yours

One of the tortoise's best friends on the islands is the Galapagos finch which helps them by eating ticks and other parasites from their body, which is also a food source for the finches. The other cool thing about the finches is that their size and beaks have evolved depending on the climate and food sources available. Two million years ago a group of finches that looked alike flew 600 miles from South America to the islands. Now the finches with long pointed beaks snatch insects, while those with broad blunt beaks crack seeds and nuts for their food.

SHORT BEAK FINCH

LONG BEAK FINCH

FELICIA THE FINCH WATCHING TABITHA THE SHORT NECKED TORTOISE

Do you believe in swimming dragons?

Galapagos is the only place in the world that has swimming lizards. These marine iguanas were forced to evolve over time because food is very scarce on the volcanic rocks.

In the morning the iguanas warm their bodies up in the sun and then the strongest and most brave plunge into the sea in search of red and white algae to eat at the bottom of the ocean. After about 10 minutes they come up to the surface and have a very hard swim back, with massive waves crashing over the rocks. On the way back to the island they also have to watch out for large sea lions who are also looking for food, maybe the unlucky iguana.

The thing you notice most is the red, yellow and bluish scales likely from the algae they eat and the dragon-like row of spikes running from their neck to the back of their tail. Like all of the Galapagos animals their size and colour vary from island to island.

How handsome are my ...

One of my favourite images is the Blue Footed Booby. It was named for the Spanish word "Bobo" which means dumb or clumsy, likely because it walks very clumsily on the rocks, but is very good at diving and fishing. The blue feet come from their diet of anchovies and sardines. The brighter blue the male feet are, the more likely they will get a mate. The males dance around on their feet to impress the females so that is how you can tell the boys from the girls. They both have long pointed wings they use to dive into the water to catch flying fish at the surface. The females usually lay one to three eggs right on the bare high ground where they can protect them from predators. They usually only end up with one healthy chick which they feed and raise and that creates the strongest chick for the next generation. I am sure glad my dog mother fed all of us, but I was the biggest in my litter anyway so most likely to survive.

GUESS WHICH ONE IS THE MALE?

the Tiniest Penguin

Another very unique bird I want to show you is the Galapagos penguin. It is the only penguin you can see north of the equator. It has adapted by becoming very small, only 14 inches long, because it is easier for smaller birds to keep cool. It lays its eggs in the tiny caves in the crevices of the volcanic rock. Penguins cannot fly and like the Boobys, they are clumsy walking on the rocks but they are great swimmers.

When the water temperatures cool down, it brings fish to eat but when it is very hot there can be a famine. The penguin will put its wings out to catch a breeze and will pant like a dog to try to cool off.

So I have something in common with the penguins!

You are what you eat!

Another beautiful bird you will see is the flamingo.
Its pretty pink and salmon colour comes from its diet of
shrimp, fishes and algae that live in the shallow coastal waters.
They have long legs, flexible necks and webbed feet (like me!)

They use their feet to stir up the mud to bring pink algae
and shrimp to the surface to snatch up and gobble.

FANNY THE FLAMINGO

OLLIE THE OYSTERCATCHER

Guess what's for dinner?

Although you can see this type of bird in parts of North and South America along the coast, the Galapagos Oystercatcher looks quite different from its ancestors. It has a long reddish beak it uses to scoop up the oysters and other shell fish and stands in the shallow water on long pinkish legs. Like many of the other Galapagos birds and lizards, its bright colours come from its diet.

One unique fact is that the Oystercatchers try to disguise their eggs from predators by placing rocks and broken shells in with their eggs. I am not sure I would like to sleep on the rocks instead of Mom and Dad's cozy bed, but then I was not born from a shell.

The best dancer award for crabs!

One of the first things you may see in the distance amongst the volcanic rock are bright orange and yellow blobs sticking out from the crevices. These are the incredible Sally Lightfoot crabs named after a nimble dancer. They have ten strong legs which allow them to move very quickly in four directions to escape their many predators and hold on to the rocks when a big wave crashes over them. They are known as the scavengers of the Galapagos, feeding on dead animals and debris laying on the rocks. My Mom does not allow me to eat dead animals in case they poison me but these crabs are made of tough stuff!

I hope you enjoyed seeing some of the amazing Galapagos animal kingdom. My Mom just read that an expedition led by Dr. Sarah Darwin, the great-great granddaughter of Charles Darwin just landed on Galapagos, packed with 200 scientists to study the animals and birds. Wouldn't it be cool to go back almost 200 years later to retrace the steps of your ancestors? I think next time Mom and Dad go to Portugal they have to take me with them, as long as I do not have to catch all of the fish for dinner.

SALLY THE SALLY LIGHTFOOT CRAB

I hope you liked sharing some of my experiences and will come with me on another walk in the wild. Who knows what amazing things we will see together.

Love, Whisky

Brenda and her husband Bob and Whisky divide their time between Toronto and Muskoka. Brenda is a recovering advertising lawyer recently inducted into the Marketing Hall of Legends. This is her fourth illustrated children's book. Art on this page by Sandy Murdy.